TIMELESS PLACES

TUSCANY

ALEXANDRA BONFANTE-WARREN

FRIEDMAN/FAIRFAX
PUBLISHERS

A FRIEDMAN/FAIRFAX BOOK
Please visit our website: www.metrobooks.com

© 2000, 1996 by Michael Friedman Publishing Group, Inc.

Library of Congress Cataloging-in-Publication Data available upon request.

ISBN 1-56799-752-X

Editor: Nathaniel Marunas
Art Director/Designer: Jeff Batzli
Photography Editor: Sarah Storey
Production Manager: Camille Lee

Color separations by Colourscan Overseas Co Pte Ltd
Printed in Hong Kong by Midas Printing Limited

3 5 7 9 10 8 6 4 2

Distributed by Sterling Publishing Company, Inc.
387 Park Avenue South
New York, NY 10016
Distributed in Canada by Sterling Publishing
Canadian Manda Group
One Atlantic Avenue, Suite 105
Toronto, Ontario, Canada M6K 3E7
Distributed in Australia by
Capricorn Link (Australia) Pty Ltd.
P.O. Box 6651
Baulkham Hills, Business Centre, NSW 2153, Australia

PAGE 1: **A misty sunrise near Montalcino silhouettes umbrella pines and cypresses, creating an unmistakably Tuscan horizon.**

PAGES 2–3: **Plague-ridden marshes in Dante Alighieri's day, the fertile fields of the Vale di Chiana, below Arezzo, were drained over subsequent centuries.**

PAGES 4–5: **Flanked by its graceful thirteenth-century** *campanile*, **the Church of Santa Maria dei Servi dreams atop one of Siena's three hilltops.
The Romanesque bell tower was heavily restored in 1926.**

FRONTISPIECE: **These hills have been farmed since the region was ruled by the splendid cities of the Etruscan federation, nearly three millennia ago.**

TITLE PAGE: **In Tuscany, home is sacred. A heavy wood** *portone* **in Siena's old quarter is warmed by the late-afternoon sun.**

Contents

RIGHT: **Cetona's steep hills rise amid some of Italy's most breathtaking panoramas. The Etruscans, often at war among themselves, built their cities—including Cetona— on easily defensible heights.**

PART I

STORIA

WARM SCENTS OF WILD ROSEMARY AND SUN-DRENCHED STRAW. THE TALL, SOMBER PILLARS OF CYPRESSES RISING MOURNFULLY OUT OF THE FLOWING LANDSCAPE. RUINED CASTLES ON HILLTOPS. MONASTERIES AND CONVENTS, AMID FIELDS AND WOODS, THEIR SIMPLE CELLS AND ARCHED CLOISTERS SHELTERING SILENCE AT THEIR HEARTS. A LANDSCAPE GLIMPSED OUT OF A VILLA TRANSPORTS US INTO THE ATMOSPHERIC BACKGROUNDS OF RENAISSANCE MASTERPIECES.

DISCREETLY LUXURIOUS, THE VILLAS AND PALAZZI OF THE COUNTRYSIDE SIT AMID LONG-TENDED GARDENS THAT EFFORTLESSLY COMBINE FORMALITY AND PLAYFULNESS. LEMON TREES IN ANTIQUE TERRA-COTTA POTS WAFT THEIR FLOWERS' HEADY SCENT DOWN ANTIQUE MAZES CLIPPED FROM BRIGHT GREEN BOX HEDGES, AROUND WHIMSICAL TOPIARY AND CLASSICAL STATUARY, AND INTO BREEZE-SWEPT, SHADED GAZEBOS OVERLOOKING WINDING LINES OF GRAPEVINES AND ROWS OF SILVERY-LEAVED OLIVE TREES.

THE CITIES BEAR THEIR LONG HISTORIES GRACEFULLY. BORN AS CITY-STATES IN ANCIENT TIMES, THEY ARE UTTERLY DISTINCT FROM ONE ANOTHER AND ARE MARKED BY INDIVIDUAL STYLES OF LIVING. THE VARIETY OF LANDSCAPE, ART, AND HISTORY THAT ABOUNDS HERE IS ASTONISHING IN A SMALL GEOGRAPHICAL AREA. PAST AND PRESENT MERGE SEAMLESSLY: LUCCA'S HIGH WALLS ARE CROWNED BY LANDSCAPED WALKS AND A TREE-SHADED AVENUE, BUILT DURING THE REIGN OF ÉLISA—ONE OF NAPOLEON'S SISTERS—WHOM THE EMPEROR MADE PRINCESS OF LUCCA AND PIOMBINO AND GRAND DUCHESS OF TUSCANY. TODAY, CARS SPEED BENEATH THE CENTURY-OLD TREES, THE DRIVERS UNAWARE, PERHAPS, OF THE GRAND DUCHESS' OWN COLORFUL HISTORY.

⚬———✦———⚬

There are traces everywhere of Tuscany's story: writing paper edged in the instantly recognizable Renaissance Florentine style (i.e., ornamented with gilt, red, and green designs) recalls the region's long tradition of learning—the University of Pisa, founded in the fourteenth century, is one of Europe's oldest universities—and diplomacy. Tuscany is the birthplace of Niccolà Machiavelli, pragmatic statesman and playwright. Leatherwork harks to the region's pastoral past, and Tuscany's celebrated gold jewelry recalls the ancient Etruscans (and, further back, Bronze and Iron Age inhabitants).

The people of Tuscany are generous, stingy, profane, pious, snobbish, and deeply democratic. They traditionally vote Communist, in keeping with a long history of collective effort and civic pride. At the same time, they are fiercely individualistic, and indeed remarkable individuals—a monk, a countess, a poet, a merchant, countless artists, and many others—influenced the destiny of the region and of Italy. The beauty, ancient and modern, of the cities and villages throughout the countryside, presents harmonious collaborations of present and past, ongoing expressions of the innate taste and balance of the remarkably attractive Tuscans.

The Tuscans are famous, too, for their *campanilismo*, a trait that is found throughout Italy in some degree. The word derives from *campanile*, or bell tower, and describes the loyalty that citizens feel for their own town above any regional or national allegiance. It is a typically Tuscan paradox that it was a Florentine, Dante Alighieri, who laid the foundation for the national language; his transcendent *Divine Comedy* was one of the first high-art European works written in the language of the people rather than in Latin.

Every city, town, and village has its own festivals. Tuscany's most famous, the Palio of Siena, is a breakneck horse race in medieval costume around the city's splendid Campo; the festival is now televised and takes place twice a year, in July and August. In July, the people of Lucca parade by torchlight in honor of Lucca's patron saint, San Paolino, and later compete in a crossbow contest.

Autumn in Tuscany means hearty harvest feasts, long rustic tables laden with the abundance of the season: tomatoes, zucchini, onions, and mushrooms, the famed beef of Tuscany, and the region's unique saltless bread, the *pane sciapo*. Everything is prepared with fresh herbs of summer—rosemary,

ABOVE: **The Palio, Siena's breakneck horse race, is probably much more ancient than the medieval costumes of the bareback riders suggest. Each neighborhood of the city fields its best—and best-looking—horsemen. The only rule is: anything goes!**

basil, and sage—gathered by the kitchen door, and with peppery, freshly pressed olive oil. Last year's wine, still new, is poured into bottles from enormous demijohns as tall as people and served up alongside the best wine of the house, which is brought up from the cellars for the occasion. Dessert is a sumptuous farewell to summer and plump last fruits: deep-flavored blackberries and succulent figs, delicious yellow plums and perfumed peaches (rich red ones as well as subtle white ones), and of course grapes, bursting and sweet beneath the protective skin. Now the canning begins, capturing the sun-warmed abundance. The jars full of nature's colors will line shelves in stone-walled rooms where herbs and hams hang from ancient rafters, bringing pleasant memories of summer into the bright, chilly days of winter.

Autumn is Tuscany's most splendid season, golden and warm, with crisp, cozy nights. This is the true high season, following as it does the dizzying summer heat, and (in Florence especially) the crush of tourists. In the cities, people return from long summer vacations at the beach, in the mountains, or abroad. Gently, summer dwindles and warm days may linger until November's downpours drive everyone indoors to

seek the pleasures of leisurely conversation and dinners spent with old friends by firelight.

In the Tuscan lowlands, by the sea and along stretches of rivers, winters are alternately mild and rainy, bright and cold. The chain of the Apennines embraces the region from northwest to southeast; high in these mountains, snow can cover peaks from December until April, and even the cities in the river valleys can receive dustings of snow. In the hills, which make up some two thirds of the Tuscan region, winds such as the legendary northern *tramontana* can be fierce, and a sudden frost can destroy centuries-old olive trees, causing grievous damage to a farm's economy (it can take eight years for a newly planted olive tree to bear fruit that is good enough to give oil).

After the last of the crops are brought in, the farmers go indoors, to mend, repair, and prepare. Some have winter jobs, some hunt. In the woods, the remnants of once-endless forests, wild boars and deer roam. Punctuated by holidays—such as Bagni di Lucca's fair in honor of the Immaculate Conception on December 8, and Viareggio's Carnival, one of Italy's most elaborate and longest festivals—winter is a time for rest before the demands of spring.

ABOVE: **The village of Sovana experienced all of Tuscany's turbulent history. The designs in the arch above this door are typical of the Lombards, who occupied northern Italy from the sixth through the eighth centuries. The stone with the human figure was recycled from an even older structure.**

ABOVE: **This view from the Rocca degli Aldobrandeschi displays the classic curved roof tiles of Tuscany, adopted and adapted the world over.**

Made of red clay, they form an elegant contrast with the lush fields below.

Spring in Tuscany is vigorous, the land thriving under exuberant showers. The specific flavor of the year's wine grapes, a combination of sturdy, delicate, and elusive, begins to form now, and will be shaped as well by the dry summer's heat, which will call forth the fruit's sugars in proportions that are unique year to year. Everywhere the myriad greens of Tuscany come to life—the young green of lawns and alfalfa, the black green of cypresses, the silver of olive trees, the placid green of chestnut trees, and the sere, desert green of the seaside umbrella pine branches atop their gnarled trunks. Much of the region's agricultural prosperity comes from the many rivers that water the hills and lowlands. Tuscany's soil, however, is in many areas almost impermeable, so heavy rains can easily cause rivers to flood. In the most recent of the big floods, in 1966, the Arno transcended its banks, pouring into Florence and causing massive destruction to homes and to irreplaceable works of art.

The landscape changes dramatically over short distances. The mountains of the west now produce marble, lead, zinc, mercury, copper, and lignite, but little is left of the iron that contributed to the region's wealth in ancient times. From the Apennines in the east spring the great rivers, most notably the Arno and the Tiber, the latter being the river of Rome. Animals live here that live nowhere else in Italy: near the border of Umbria, a few last wolves and wildcats still prowl, though no bears have been seen since the 1700s. The fertile hills, with their secret vales and thick woods, give way to undulating fields. The first wheat springs up, dotted with orange-red poppies, their petals as fragile as a butterfly's wings. Mustard

fills fields with yellow-tipped stalks, and bold sunflowers reach for the sun. The patterned fields seem a part of the land itself, as organic as the crests of the Apennines or the rocks of Il Giglio off the coast. And indeed this fruitful land has been tilled for millennia and inhabited since Paleolithic times.

The first to plant crops and pasture sheep were the people of the Neolithic age, some five or six thousand years ago. Their successors, the folk of the so-called Apenninic Bronze Age, from about 1,500 to 1,000 B.C.E., left marvelous incised vases and sophisticated tools of stone, bone, and metal. The local copper made the manufacture of these bronze vessels possible, and drove much of the trade that enriched the region. The people of the later Bronze Age began to build their small settlements on hilltops, making them more easily defended than their earlier riverside hamlets.

In the Iron Age, the mines of the west, especially on the island of Elba, were rich in that then-precious metal; the area's silver mines further enhanced the region's prosperity. In the eighth century B.C.E., however, a singular people emerged that would leave their mark indelibly on history. They called themselves Rasna, but the Romans called them Etrusci, or Tusci, and their land—from the Arno to the Tiber—Etruria or Tuscia. (Tuscany today, though somewhat smaller, is essentially the area it was in the eighth century B.C.E.)

Like their descendants, the Etruscans loved decoration, and their tomb paintings display in vivid colors a daily life that at least the aristocrats vastly enjoyed. Their terra-cotta sculpture displays a sureness, sensuality, and immediacy that contrasts with the sober artistry of their neighbors the Greeks, and their skill in working gold would remain unmatched until the Renaissance. Their scandalous lifestyle shocked the Greeks and later the Romans, too—the Etruscan women actually banqueted with their men! By the third century B.C.E., internal wars among the Etruscan cities, a class system no longer suited to the times, and Roman might subdued these gifted artists, soothsayers, and merchants. Rome absorbed Etruria, and now only that people's art remains. That, and the occasional face in a crowd....

Following the collapse of the Roman Empire of the West in the fifth century C.E., Tuscany suffered devastating waves of invaders from the north. Cities were destroyed—some never to rise again—and many of the region's inhabitants fled, abandoning farms and villages. The coast was easy prey for Saracen raiders, and the *maremme*, the marshlands near the sea, became malarial, so that the western shore was also virtually deserted. In the eighth century, however, the region was incorporated into Charlemagne's Frankish empire, which in time provided some stability and security. This stability nurtured the cities back to life, restoring them to their primordial functions as marketplaces, especially as trade with the Near East increased.

Some of the major landlords were monasteries. The Benedictine monasteries, in particular, disciplined and well-organized, were dedicated to self-sufficiency and thus to working the land. Their sometimes vast holdings employed many laypeople and also countered the social fragmentation that the feudal system promoted. In time, some of the monasteries became wealthy and worldly political forces. In reaction

to that, reformed houses were founded. One of the most important of these, the Camaldolese Benedictines, originated in Tuscany.

A new movement was forming in the reemerging cities. Inspired in part by a new religious fervor, they were taking sides in the widening rift between papacy and empire that was blazing across Europe, forcing precarious alliances and often murderous partisanships. At the same time, the Crusades were stimulating trade, which revived coastal cities such as Pisa, but also encouraged local textile manufacturers and the fledgling banking industry in Florence and Siena. The rich merchant families began to create dynasties through intermarriage with the aristocracy, often poor nobles who were happy to trade their ancient names for the power and riches the onetime tradesmen commanded. Soon Tuscan merchants were living as the nobility did elsewhere, commissioning public and religious buildings as well as the staggering quantity of fine art for which Tuscany is known throughout the world.

By the early 1400s, Florence dominated much of Tuscany. The relative peace that settled over a region so long lacerated by factionalism coincided with a resurgence of interest in the classical authors of Greece and Rome—the Renaissance. Inspired by Roman ideals, prosperous trading families began to build simple but elegant villas in the now-tranquil Tuscan countryside.

Side by side with the increasingly aristocratic tradesmen, the artists' guilds were energetic and effective civic groups that contributed to the balance of power, if not democracy, that characterized many Tuscan cities. Resuming the traditions of the metalworking Etruscans, Tuscan goldsmiths became celebrated throughout Europe. Sandro Botticelli was only one of numerous artists who trained with goldsmiths, and many artists were in fact the children of goldsmiths. The prosperity of the citizens and guilds was expressed in private and public works of devotional art, as well as portraits celebrating individuals and dynastic alliances, all of it of a quality that would set a standard throughout Europe for centuries.

The Medicis' influence was recognized by the European powers with the conferral of the title of duke of Florence, which was bestowed upon Cosimo I in 1537. When the title of grand duke of Tuscany was granted Cosimo I by Pope Pius V in 1569, Tuscany was once more united (though the republic of Lucca was to remain independent, even if not always a republic, until it joined the newly forming kingdom of Italy in 1860). The Medicis would twice marry into the French royal family. In 1533, Catherine married Henry II; Italians maintain, with good reason, that she created French haute cuisine

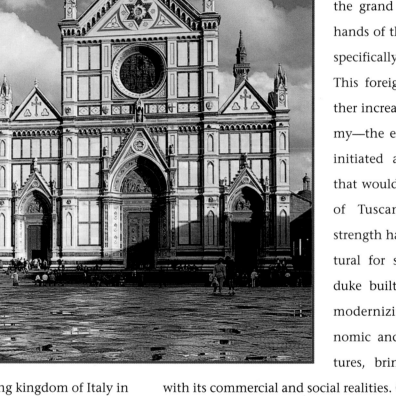

when she brought her own personal chefs with her to her husband's court.

In the following century, Tuscany, now a major power, joined the Holy League against the Turks, who would not be finally defeated in Europe until well into the 1700s. In 1737, the last of the Medicis died, and the grand duchy came into the hands of the Hapsburg-Lorraines, specifically to their second sons. This foreign dynasty would further increase the region's autonomy—the energetic Peter Leopold initiated a number of reforms that would become characteristic of Tuscan life. The region's strength had been chiefly agricultural for some time; the grand duke built on that strength by modernizing the region's economic and administrative structures, bringing them into line with its commercial and social realities. Countering late Medici policies, he sustained the rights of the state in the face of the church's authority. His support of the controversial bishop of Pistoia led to tumultuous uprisings in the last years of his life,

ABOVE: **The Church of Santa Croce, or the Holy Cross, in Florence, was begun in the thirteenth century and completed in the nineteenth. It was intended as a preaching church—the square in front was meant to accommodate the devout who could not fit inside.**

but his enlightened civic changes set Tuscany apart from its less progressive neighbors, in Italy and in Europe generally.

For the first fifteen years of the nineteenth century, Tuscany was absorbed into the French empire; ironically, it was Napoleon who instituted the short-lived "kingdom of Etruria." The region's turbulent international political vicissitudes ended with the unification of Italy in 1861, though its passionate commitment to freedom endures—during World War II, for example, the Tuscans were notoriously fierce partisans of the anti-Nazi Resistance. The region was the site of some of the most bitter fighting during that war, and Florence, Pisa, and Leghorn were especially damaged by the bombings.

In the late eighteenth century, a fashion began that endures under other guises today. Napoleon's conquest of Egypt, as well as excavations in southern Italy, had inspired a neoclassical fever among members of the British aristocracy. Italy in general, and Tuscany in particular, became requisite stops on the Grand Tour, considered necessary to add a finish of culture to the future leaders of England. In addition, the region's mild climate and its relative tolerance in social matters appealed to those members of the British upper class who for various reasons were no longer welcome in society. Tuscany's limitless medieval treasures drew the second generation of Romantics, Europeans, and Americans who came to admire San Gimignano's sensual frescoes, Siena's golden pieces of heaven, and Volterra's ancient turnings.

For thousands of years, people have been drawn to this part of the world, first by its fertile soil, then by the wealth beneath it. A unique marriage of shrewd commerce, worldly pride, and passionate spirituality produced an outpouring of genius that resonates still today. Like their forebears through the centuries, today's travelers are bewitched by Tuscany's rolling landscapes, snow-capped mountains, and sea-washed rocks. But most of all they are enchanted by the mystery of life and art entwined—the art of life.

Cities

Tuscany is known for the beauty of its landscape, but far more for the splendid explosion of art and architecture that began in the late Middle Ages and flourished gloriously during the Renaissance. Ironically, in much of the region, the medieval sections of the cities were razed in the nineteenth century for the construction that the expanding population required. Yet, in large and small cities alike, a visitor turns a corner and is suddenly transported back five hundred years or more. Walking down narrow streets between these two- and three-story brick houses the color of wine, a visitor experiences the sweep of those distant centuries.

What strikes travelers is the rich variety of the cities, their mysterious but palpable individuality. Many of these cities have been lived in for three thousand years or more, and their identities reflect these ancient roots. Festivals still proliferate throughout the year in every corner of this region, commemorating patron saints, historical or seasonal events, or moments now lost to time. Arezzo's Joust of the Saracen, for example, may hark back to as early as the ninth and tenth centuries, when North African Arabs occupied Sicily and invaded the mainland, or to the years of the Crusades.

ABOVE: **Siena's sinuous streets are here seen from the Torre del Mangia. The body of the tower, which derived its name from that of its first bell-ringer, Mangiaguadagni, or "Earnings-eater," is made of terra-cotta crowned with stone.**

Attracted by the many rivers, dense woodlands, and fertile plains and hillsides, people have lived in the region now known as Tuscany since the earliest Stone Age. While these people lived by the rivers, the Etruscans built their cities inland (out of reach of their fellow pirates) and on hilltops, for better defense. The mountains provided stone for construction, and the endless forests gave them wood for building homes and ships and for fueling the forges that produced metalwork superior to anything in the peninsula. In the watered valleys and on their terraced hills, the people grew grains, grapevines, olive trees, and flax, from which they made linen. They raised cattle and traded objects and ideas with other peoples of the Mediterranean and Aegean. Still today, their frescoes, sculpture, and jewelry stand out for their elegance and for the stunning skill with which they were fashioned. The Etruscans were an imaginative, creative people,

renowned for their augury, or fortune-telling (primarily reading the flights of birds or the livers of sacrificed animals). Related to this skill was their reputed magical ability to draw the boundaries of cities in such a way as to attract good fortune; according to legend, for instance, Romulus consulted the Etruscans when he was ready to plow the ritual furrow that would determine the perimeter of Rome.

Like the Greeks, the Etruscans had a system of city-states, which developed more or less individualistically, and were often at war among themselves, in a series of shifting alliances that also included non-Etruscans. Although by the end of the seventh century B.C.E., the Etruscans ruled Rome, their power declined rapidly during the following centuries. In the fifth century B.C.E., the Greek fleet from Syracuse, in Sicily, destroyed the Etruscan fleet, and by the fourth century B.C.E., Roman expansionism was enveloping Etruscan cities. In the

ABOVE: **Portoferraio, the capital of Elba, retains the word for "iron," recalling the island's ancient importance as a rich source of that metal. The town was also home to Napoleon from May 1814 to February 1815.**

second century C.E., many of the Etruscan cities north of Rome were devastated, and the land, once infinitely prosperous, was now left barren, as the low cost of Egyptian grain undermined the region's agriculture.

In the centuries after the fall of the Roman Empire, the cities of Tuscia, as the region was then called, suffered barbarian invasions from the north. The cities were destroyed by outsiders or abandoned by their terrified inhabitants. During the Lombard occupation of the sixth century C.E., Lucca, the home of the ruling marquess, was the region's principal city, though Pisa, as the Lombards' naval port, was also important. The other cities of the west were virtually deserted, in part because of the now endemic malaria and, beginning in the eighth century, because of Arab attacks from the sea.

Under Charlemagne and then the Frankish kings, previously secondary cities such as Pistoia, Florence, Arezzo, and Siena began to grow. In the following centuries, Lucca and Pisa, as might be expected, began to emerge as political forces, but so, for the first time, did Florence. This strengthening of the cities was greatest in the cities that housed a bishop, for it was in this period that one of Tuscany's determining phases took shape.

The death, in 814, of Charlemagne was the beginning of the Holy Roman Empire, giving birth to a ruthless struggle over the temporal power of the Roman Catholic Church in Europe. In the eleventh and twelfth centuries a Benedictine monk and a Tuscan countess would influence the destinies of the cities of Tuscany. The Benedictine monk rose to become Pope (later Saint) Gregory VII, who in the eleventh century reformed the church and vigorously maintained its political as well as spiritual preeminence. The countess was Matilda of Tuscany, La Gran Contessa, who bequeathed her vast possessions to the pope. The countess and the pope had a common enemy in the Holy Roman emperor Henry IV, who had been responsible for her father's murder.

Like most rulers of her day, Matilda traveled constantly throughout her possessions; in her absence, groups of notables governed her cities. The countess' legacy was twofold. First, the towns, having developed the habit of self-government, adopted the civic organization of the commune, and soon became powerful themselves. Second, Tuscany, town by town, became central in the murderous feud that blazed between the papacy and the Holy Roman emperors.

These two factions—the Guelphs, who supported the popes, and the Ghibellines, on the side of the emperors—were at odds for centuries, with cities often switching sides and alliances, much as their Etruscan forebears had done. Dante Alighieri, author of the *Divine Comedy*, was forced to leave his beloved Florence as a result of these squabbles, and ultimately died in exile. The rift between pope and emperor only exacerbated the cities' ongoing and brutal attempts to conquer other Tuscan cities in order to increase their land (or, in the case of Florence's war against Pisa, to have a port to facilitate trade). These bloody struggles went on not only between cities, but within them. San Gimignano is famous for its towers, but most of the cities of Tuscany had similar skylines, as families raised fortress-like houses to protect themselves against their neighbors.

In the midst of some of the cruelest warfare the world has ever seen, the fervent faith of the time inspired the creation of works of art as well as the architecture that housed them. The broad vaulted arches of the Romanesque style left lavish wall space to be filled by frescoes that narrated the miracles of saints, the nightmare terrors of Hell, and the pleasures of Heaven that were beyond imagining. Giotto's figures, revolutionary for their time, express intense human emotions, their faces creased in anguish, their gestures bespeaking grief or solemnity.

By the 1300s, Florence was Tuscany's superpower—cash, as much as military might, accounted for Florence's hegemony. It had razed neighboring Fiesole to the ground two centuries before, and now it held Arezzo, San Gimignano, Volterra, and Cortona, among others. In 1406, Pisa came into Florence's political and economic orbit as well. Some local festivals still recall in their ferocious factionalism some of the passion of those days. Siena's Palio, for example, is a reckless bareback horse race in which the jockeys represent the *contrade*, or neighborhoods. The competition arouses venal, violent, and ecstatic emotions for months before its culmination in July and August.

Strolling through San Gimignano and the medieval sections of Arezzo, Volterra, and Cortona today, it is hard to imagine that Florence, in the fifteenth century one of the largest cities in Italy (or for that matter, Europe), numbered some 100,000 inhabitants. Florence had more painters than butchers (in part because there were few butchers—cooking did not yet call for specialized cuts of meat), and when the papacy returned to Rome after the period of Avignon, it was primarily the artists of Tuscany whom the popes summoned to decorate the Vatican.

The cities of Tuscany are vigorous works of art, overflowing with history, mystery, and beauty, but also *gelaterie*, markets, and movie theaters. Every city, town, and village boasts churches, cloisters, piazze, and palazzi that are and contain some of the most splendid expressions of the human spirit ever created by hand and mind. But such wonders are vital to the fabric of these cities, and when we open our hearts to these visions, we, too, become part of that magical tapestry of art and life.

Countryside

In a country lane, the crimson-throated white blossoms of pomegranate bushes are shockingly exotic amid the familiar fig trees, their black fruit nestling heavy behind leaves broader than a person's hand, and the gleaming blue-purple of blackberries, their thorny vines draping over sturdy, weather-worn fences. Plucked as they grow, these warm, still-living fruits are tangibly vital.

In northern Tuscany, striped fields of wheat alternate with dense, dark copses of ancient trees; rows of grapevines, the clusters of grapes absorbing the low, slanting rays of early autumn; and lines of gnarled olive trees, their long, slender leaves flirting silver between the low, rich blue of the sky and the straw-colored soil. In the north, the land is more dramatic, its rolling hills home to secret glens where once the early people of these places worshiped now-nameless gods.

ABOVE: **The severe verticals of the cypresses echo the towers of nearby San Gimignano. Equally well known is the town's vernaccia, a popular white wine.**

In the south, the land is flatter, like long ocean waves. Sudden circular hillocks crown rises. Some of these small hills conceal Etruscan tombs still to be excavated, in the ongoing reconciliation of past and present. Fields of shy yellow mustard and bold yellow sunflowers are newcomers to this region, yet the Tuscan landscape takes all in, folding the new into the ancient, endlessly.

At the height of the Etruscan era, the area's wealthiest families owned extensive, bountiful tracts of land, often worked by slave hands. As Etruscan might disintegrated and ultimately vanished, the lands were inefficiently farmed by Roman soldier-colonists who were more political place-holders than true farmers. It seems impossible that this countryside could ever have been different than this, beneath the low, eternal sky. Yet Plutarch reported that Tiberius Gracchus was moved to seek agrarian reform when he witnessed the devastated, abandoned farms of Etruria. Despite the emperor Augustus' attempts to revive the once-flourishing land, it remained untilled during the long centuries of the barbarian invasions.

In those centuries, industry declined, and the cities with it. In the economic chaos, powerful families settled or stole large landholdings, seeking, like their neighbors dedicated to the religious life, to provide for themselves in the virtual absence of trade. Those who worked these lands were nominally free, though they could not leave the land. They were serfs, the lowest on the chain of classes forming the feudal system, which in turn fragmented the land of Tuscany and gave rise to a period of almost incessant warfare.

Nestled along the twisting roads of the Tuscan hills are monasteries and convents that have been receiving travelers within their tranquil walls for centuries. Some of these convents are still active religious communities, hosting a few guests in pristine surroundings, while others have been converted to (often lavish) hotels and gourmet restaurants. So at home are these structures in the Tuscan landscape that we remember with surprise that monasticism originated in Egypt and Syria. Fleeing the Roman persecutions, the monks and their movement migrated west. One of these communities of monks, in central Italy, drafted

ABOVE: **A monk strolls in contemplation near Monte Oliveto Maggiore, home of the imposing Benedictine abbey that was one of the most famous monuments of Tuscany's golden age.**

a holy isolate, one Benedict of Norcia, to be its abbot. His legend relates a detail that says much about central Italy in the early sixth century. Benedict desired to build a church from a temple to the god Apollo, which had been worshiped at by the Etruscans, Greeks, and Romans for more than a thousand years. The Devil sat on a stone, making it so heavy that the brothers could not lift it; Benedict made the sign of the cross over it, and they were able to move it easily. This story reminds us that paganism (literally, "the religion of the countryside") and Christianity coexisted for centuries.

The Benedictine monks worked the surrounding fields, but in time the monasteries employed farmers from the area. They were immensely successful economic units, and also provided social stability amid the patchwork warfare around them. As the feudal system gave way to the resurgence of the cities, the monasteries continued as viable systems for hundreds of years more.

Handsome ocher-walled villas, roofed in the curved, overlapping red tiles of Tuscany, dot the landscape, each one set in gardens and surrounded by sometimes hundreds of acres of cultivated land. But in the woods are the wild boars that are a

menace to crops, and the prey of hunters. Sitting at dusk with a family of *contadini*, the sophisticated descendants of the proud Tuscan peasants, a visitor can still hear a tale of the merciful recovery of a favorite dog, gored by the deadly tusks of a wild sow protecting her young, hidden in the forest underbrush.

The farming system of *mezzadria*—from the word for "half"—established in the Middle Ages brings to mind the North American misery known as share-cropping. In Tuscany, as elsewhere, this system could in difficult times easily ruin a farming family. The economic risks were great: the Tuscan land is wonderfully fertile, but it absorbs water unpredictably, making farming even more hazardously dependent upon the vagaries of the weather than usual. Nevertheless, the system of mezzadria allowed the contadini to be autonomous, to develop the independence for which they are known today.

The system was legally abolished in the 1970s. The "economic miracle" that occurred in Italy in those years extended to the countryside as well, where new mechanical and chemical technology replaced outdated agricultural mainstays, such as ox-drawn plows and carts, which in some cases harked back

ABOVE: **A romantic fresco of pastoral life decorates a wall in a private home, the Villa di Geggiano, in Siena.**

to prehistoric times. In fact, these methods are sometimes still the most practical, and persist on farms along the back roads, amid even the most advanced machinery.

Nothing is new under the Tuscan sun. Many of the large landowners of Tuscany have gone into industry, leaving the villas empty. As they did a hundred years ago, foreigners come to visit, and many of them come to stay, renting or buying these villas and the *casoni*, the frescoed farmhouses built for the signori of the last century. Now these transplanted inhabitants walk through the vineyards and olive groves with the contadini, learning more than simply the words for things as they take in the ancient enchantment of these hills and forests, of a countryside whose beauty continues to triumph over the whims and winds of history.

The Sea

The Tuscan coast, rarely visited except by Tuscans, is an essential part of the region's identity and history. From loud, jolly, overbuilt resort towns, such as Viareggio and Forte dei Marmi (literally "fortress of the marble quarries"), with their sandy beaches, to the aristocratic havens of Ansedonia, Porto Santo Stefano, and the rocky islands of the archipelago, to the Maremma, with its piney stretches of reclaimed marshland, this area is one of the most varied in Italy.

The Maremma was still wholesome during the Roman Empire, but began to silt up. During the centuries of barbarian invasions, the area became desolate, and eventually deadly, malarial swamps. In the early Middle Ages, the Cistercians were instrumental in beginning to drain the marshlands, an effort that was continued by the Medici lords in the sixteenth century. One of the many public works effected by Peter Leopold in the eighteenth century was the further draining of these lands, a project that would be revived and finally completed in the 1930s.

The Maremma and the other coastal lowlands; Elba; and the islands of the Tuscan archipelago share some of the vegetation of the region's hills and plains. On the steep, sharp slopes of the Isola del Giglio, grapevines produce Ansonaco, the island's famous wine, while olive, fig, and chestnut trees and pines recall their inland cousins. The *macchia*, however, is a forbidding underbrush of arid, virtually impenetrable scrub that is found only on the islands of the Mediterranean. During periods of revolt, the macchia provided a secure cover for rebels.

Even in antiquity, the origins of the Etruscans were debated. Though one classical authority believed them to be indigenous to Italy, most ancient historians believed them to be seafaring people, probably Lydians, from what is today Turkey. According to tradition, shortly before the Trojan War the Lydians suffered a famine so severe that half the population was ordered to emigrate so that those who remained would be able to eat. The emigrants would have followed King Tyrrhenos, and for this reason the Greeks called the Etruscans "Tyrrhenians," and named after them the sea that bordered their land and that they plied as traders (some say as pirates).

The Etruscans were as talented in commerce as they were in art and manufacturing, and were also a formidable naval power—Egyptian documents of the thirteenth and twelfth centuries B.C.E. refer to an attempted amphibious invasion, and it is very likely that one of the "sea peoples" who attacked was the Etruscans.

The Mediterranean and Aegean seas were heavily traveled in ancient times, and the line between trade and piracy was not always clear—for defensive reasons, most of the Etruscan cities were inland. Populonia is one of the few Etruscan cities to be built near the sea, along with Piombino, the important metal-forging city located amid the mines of western Etruria.

With the relative peace that resulted from the Romanization of Italy, the ruling classes built villas on the coastline as well as on such islands as Giannutri, originally named after the Roman goddess Diana, where ruins of Roman villas and baths survive on the tiny one–square mile (2.62square km) half-moon-shaped rock. Giannutri shared much of the mainland's history: from the tenth century, for example, it was occupied by Cistercian monks, members of one of the orders that sprang up in reaction to the corruption of the Benedictine ideals. And during Pisa's heyday, the rock served as a base for the city's commercial shipping.

In the early Middle Ages, Pisa achieved a brief—by historic standards—but spectacular supremacy among the coastal cities. During the Crusades it developed into a wealthy commercial port, and its ships carried troops to the Holy Land. Soon, with Genoa and Venice, it shrewdly had taken advantage of its experience in the Near East to become one of the most powerful trading cities in the Mediterranean. Like Genoa and Venice, Pisa had prosperous colonies on the Near Eastern coasts, and the naval muscle to support them. Pisa not only successfully resisted Arab incursions, but in the eleventh century the city liberated Sardinia from the Saracens' three-hundred-year hold on the island. Its population at the time is estimated to have been around 150,000, a staggering number for the time.

Pisa also profited from its Ghibelline partisanship: in 1162 the emperor granted the city an important stretch of the coast south toward Rome, and later the island of Sardinia in fief. The city's wealth went into its churches and into the support of art intended to inspire the faithful with desire for Heaven and a fear of Hell. Like a medieval morality play, though, Pisa began to decline even as it was reaching its peak.

ABOVE: **In the gentle fishing village of Santo Stefano, not all of the technology is motorized....**

Too many external and internal conflicts were weakening the city, and before the end of the 1200s, its former ally Genoa virtually destroyed Pisa's fleet at Leghorn. Without its fleet, the city, no longer capable of either conducting its trade or defending its colonies, soon subsided into history. In 1406, succumbing to a long siege, it was absorbed into the Florentine "empire."

Leghorn (in Italian, Livorno) dates to at least 904; in the following century it boasted a castle. In the fourteenth century, the area belonged to Pisa, but was to become the crowning urban and mercantile project of the Medici grand dukes. In less than a century, under Cosimo I, his sons, and Cosimo II, Livorno grew and blossomed. What gave the city its great economic impetus and singular personality was an unusual provision: it was a free port, open to foreign ships and goods, but even more importantly, it was open to foreigners, including non-Catholics. In sixteenth- and seventeenth-century Europe, this meant that Greeks, people of the Near East, and Protestants (chiefly British and Dutch), but most of all, Jews, whose civic status in the various states of Europe often depended upon the goodwill of specific rulers, were able to use the port. At Livorno, religious toleration, being a matter of economic policy, was somewhat more reliable. The Jewish community of Livorno thrived, although this meant that during the German occupation of 1943–44, it was the target of Nazi sweeps. The Jewish population was decimated, but

ABOVE: **Once virtually deserted, the Maremma has become a prosperous agricultural and mineral region, and host to a string of thriving beach resorts.**

many returned after the war, re-creating what is today a significant community.

The Medici policy was a success, and by the end of the 1700s, Livorno was the second city of Tuscany, after Florence. Since Unification, in 1861, Livorno has continued as a successful traditional port, but has also flourished with important contemporary industries in the metal, mechanical, and chemical sectors.

Fine

The sailors and armies of Tuscany took the goods of the region (its silk and gold pieces, especially) across the sea to the wider world, but Tuscany's real treasures were left behind—not only in the churches and palazzi of the cities, but throughout the countryside and along the rocky coasts. The land itself is an ancient canvas: on forbidding, marmoreal shores, a long-ago people who prayed to distant gods landed in fear and hope among strangers, and thrived; in intimate settlements nestled throughout the countryside, Roman conquerors took their ease amid burbling fountains; and across the plains to the north and to the east turbaned and towheaded invaders alike stormed the area in the name of yet another god, in search of gold, or wine, or any of the countless comforts of a leisured civilization. In the end each visitor as well as each settler contributed to the spirit of one of the most beautiful and romantic locations on earth.

ABOVE: **The vineyards of Montalcino yield one of the world's most prized red wines, brunello, so called for its almost earth-brown tint.**

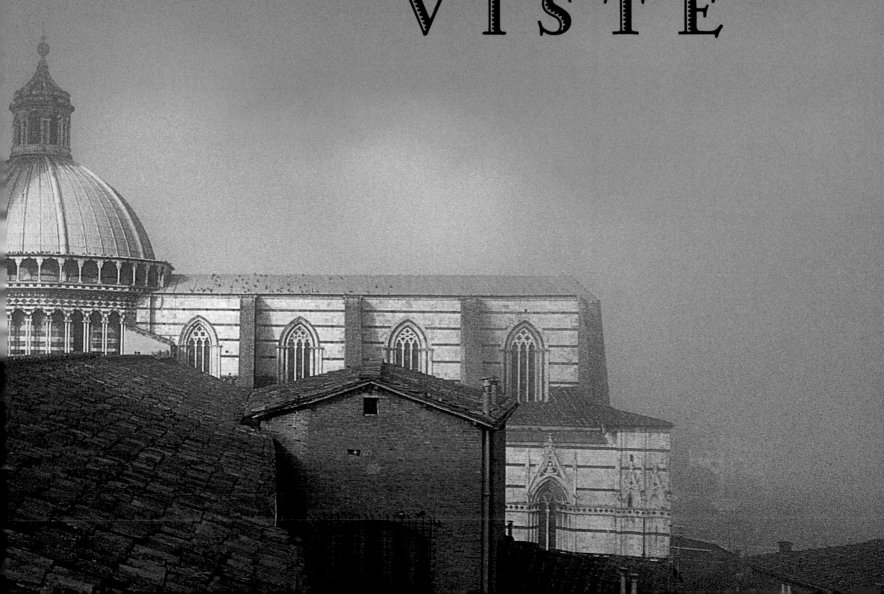

PART II

VISTE

PAGES 32–33: **Dedicated to the Virgin of the Assumption, the serene grandeur of the Duomo of Siena is unmistakable. It was begun in 1196 on the site of an earlier church, and in 1339 plans, later abandoned, were made to triple the size of the Duomo. The sculpted façade is both ornate and majestic, revealing a sophisticated use of local red and green marble.**

LEFT: **Typically, country houses are built to the edge of the road, and these on a curve in Cutigliano, in northern Tuscany, are true to form. The area is a popular resort in both summer, when the hills catch welcome breezes, and winter, when the slopes attract skiers from all over Italy.**

ABOVE: **This tree-lined avenue is actually the top of Lucca's massive walls, raised between 1504 and 1645. In the first half of the nineteenth century, Marie-Louise de Bourbon di Parma, Napoleon's second wife and (eventual) widow, landscaped the walls in an enduring gesture of peace.**

ABOVE: **"Fuel"** reads the sign beside this modest business establishment in Lucca. This might mean coal, wood, or gas in cylinders. Although Tuscany is one of the most advanced regions in one of the industrialized nations of the world, progress is still often considered optional....

ABOVE: **To enter Volterra is to walk into the Middle Ages, but there is a feeling in its sun-warmed streets of even earlier ages, perhaps the sensual trace of the Etruscans' fierce passion for life.**

ABOVE: **Public and private. Shutters in Siena keep rooms cool within thick walls.**

RIGHT: **A boar's head decorates a fountain built in 1931 in Alberese.**

FAR RIGHT: **A priest walks his parish, an image that could belong to any age in Tuscany's history.**

ABOVE: **At its heart, Florence is a city made to be lived in, as this charming, time-worn façade attests. The Italian virtue of *bella figura* ("looking good") does not always extend to the outside of a house, because it's what's inside—home and family—that counts.**

ABOVE: **In Tuscany, professionals are more and more frequently renovating houses in the *quartieri popolari*, or "working-class neighborhoods."**
As this colorful juxtaposition shows, Tuscans effortlessly blend the old and the new into a seamless whole.

OPPOSITE: **Much of medieval Florence was torn down in the nineteenth century to make way for new construction. This intimate view contrasts a lamp from the nineteenth century and the façade of Florence's magnificent Duomo, the Cathedral of Santa Maria del Fiore—the Virgin of the Flower.**

RIGHT: **The Duomo was originally conceived to overshadow the cathedrals of Pisa and Siena. Its style, severe and opulent, mysterious and magnificent, harmonizes Giotto's campanile and Filippo Brunelleschi's dome. The dome's architect is the only person buried in the cathedral.**

RIGHT: The cold weather brings a few snow-falls a year, gently dusting Tuscan homes, churches, and walls. A half hour from Siena, Montepulciano, one of the highest of Tuscany's hill towns, is also one of the region's most elegant; its landscape in spring inspired Botticelli's allegorical painting of that season, and the area boasts some of Italy's, and thus the world's, most perfect Renaissance architecture. Here, a campanile rises from a sea of Tuscan red tile, serenely surveying a tumble of broad-based medieval houses, aristocratic fifteenth- and sixteenth-century palazzi, and the handsome walls that Antonio di Sangallo the Elder built in 1511 for Cosimo I. Host to a celebrated international jazz festival, Montepulciano is known locally for its ancient local theatrical tradition. The town is most famous for its aptly named vino nobile, "ennobled" by Pope Pius III's wine steward, who declared it "a wine for lords." After the crops have been brought in and the grapes harvested from the slopes below the town, Montepulciano turns inward, to winter dreams.

BELOW: Pienza, designed as a model of Renaissance urban planning,
still inspires conversation and thoughtful reflection.

RIGHT: **A produce stand in the village of Abbadia San Salvatore, which was founded as an abbey town in the eighth century and was sold to Siena in the fourteenth. As this view shows, the agricultural products of the region are as critical to life in Tuscany today as they were when such towns as this kept agriculture alive during the devastating Germanic invasions of the Middle Ages.**

RIGHT: **Ocher, a kind of clay, exists in nature in almost twenty hues. Three of these hues adorn these simple yet elegant homes in Pisa, once one of the most powerful cities in Europe.**

PAGES 50–51: **The elegant Renaissance cloister of Prato's Church of San Francesco makes spring a private pleasure.**

RIGHT:
Wisteria pours down the fieldstone walls of this country home in Cortona. Nestled on the western slopes of the Apennines, the town displays architecture related to that of nearby Umbria.

ABOVE:
The carefully ordered chaos of the climbers surrounding this window in Saturnia demonstrates just how committed to living with nature Tuscans are. Saturnia, in southern Tuscany, is believed to have been founded by the original Italic inhabitants, well before the Etruscans—its name honors the national god of Italy. Its natural sulfur springs make it as popular now as it was three thousand years ago.

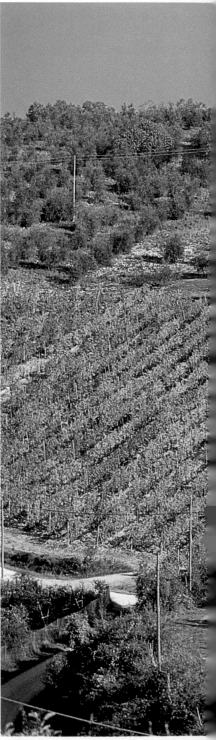

ABOVE: **An old *casale*, or "farmhouse," near San Gimignano shows off its severe but graceful proportions amid the soft hills of central Tuscany.**

RIGHT: **Chianti, just outside Florence, is world-famous for its wine; the area's olive oil, which also has its vintages, is equally prized. This soil has been producing these great things for millennia.**

LEFT: **This landscape could only be in Tuscany. Monte San Quirico is north of Lucca, but this stand of cypresses could be from any Tuscan place and time.**

ABOVE AND OPPOSITE: **An olive tree, one of the icons of Tuscany, can live to be hundreds, even thousands, of years old—generations of farmers often know every tree in their orchards. With time, the trunks grow thicker, the outlines more individual. The fierce winter storms from the mountains sometimes wreak serious damage on crops and farms. It can take as many as eight years for a new tree to produce fruit.**

LEFT: Olives are harvested in early to mid-November. When the moment has come, they must be picked immediately, often into the night, either by hand or by beating the branches with sticks to shake the fruit loose. After harvesting, the olives are taken to the nearby *frantoio*, where they will be pressed for oil. The first pressing produces the most flavorful green oil, used at the hearty feast, accompanied by generous pourings of local wine, that celebrates the *raccolta*, or "harvest."

LEFT: **The contadini, "country folk," of Tuscany are anything but provincial, and farm chores are no excuse for not being fashionable.**

ABOVE: In the autumn, the harvest is prepared for winter use. The tops of onions are braided, then dried in the autumn sun, creating garlands that will decorate farmhouse kitchens during the cold months. Red onions are found throughout Tuscan cuisine, whether adding a succulent bite to the flavorful summer bread salad, *panzanella*, or garnishing white beans *all'uccelletto*.

FAR LEFT: *Pane toscano*, the characteristic Tuscan bread made without salt, is bought fresh every day. LEFT: As every gardener knows, when the tomato crop comes in, it comes in bushels. Different ways of drying produce different flavors to bring color and taste into winter dishes. Tomatoes can be hung like herbs in a cool, dry place or set out to allow the sun to enhance the intense essence of the fruit. BOTTOM: *Ribollita*, meaning "twice-boiled," is an impeccable variable blend of the simple and the sophisticated: in this case, a savory vegetable stew, featuring fresh beans.

OPPOSITE: **Giotto was born not far from this tiny chapel, near Vicchio. This peaceful area was the site of a ruthless battle between the Florentine Guelphs and the imperial troops.**

ABOVE: **A bench to sit on in the sun, an overhang to shelter a meal with friends—this rustic shed belongs to a prosperous farm, whose more groomed house and garden are just across the way.**

OPPOSITE: **As suggestive as the background in a painting by Leonardo da Vinci—a son of Tuscany—this foggy landscape displays a rich and subtle palette of shades of green.**

ABOVE: **The autumn light in this vineyard near Stia, in the Casentino north of Arezzo, carries within it the red of the late grape leaves.**

ABOVE: **Tuscans have little reputation for whimsy, but delight in the abundant grape harvest at Antinori's Santa Cristina vineyards in Chianti has prompted a decoration for the oxen, a small gesture that may be as ancient as the land itself—or as the worship of bulls.**

BELOW: **The proper barrels, or *botte*, are crucial to the wine-making process. Here, coopers in San Casciano, in Chianti, build the containers in which the pressed juice will age properly.**

ABOVE AND LEFT: **Grapes must be harvested by hand—and at the exact moment when the balance between sugars and acidity is achieved. The mysterious chemistry of the seasons determines each year's complex of flavors—each vintage is as individual as the year itself is.**

ABOVE: **The crushed grapes go though an initial fermentation in open vats; from there they are transferred to demijohns or wood vats, depending upon the size of the vineyard. There are at least twenty labels of brunello, which can be one of the world's best wines.**

PAGES 72–73: **Symmetrical rows of trees planted for pulp are an innovation of this century.**

LEFT: **As in all agricultural traditions, nothing is wasted. Tuscans tend to be conservative, frugal, and uncharmed by novelty for novelty's sake; at the same time, they have been able to find ways to keep traditional crafts, such as basket weaving, economically viable.**

TOP: **One of Christopher Columbus's enduring contributions to Italian cuisine was corn, from which polenta, a staple of north and south alike, is made. Cornmeal is poured slowly into boiling water, stirred patiently, then either served ladled golden from the cauldron or poured out to cool on a board, then cut into pieces to be fried, broiled, or baked.**

BOTTOM: **Tuscany manages to keep life human-scale; here, wheat is separated from its chaff in a precious moment of intimate contact between generations.**

LEFT: **The emperor Augustus claimed that he found Rome built of brick and left it in marble, and indeed, the quarries of Carrara, in northwestern Tuscany, have provided marble for sculptors and architects for thousands of years. The quarries export half a million metric tons a year throughout the world, and the Carrara stoneworkers are as renowned as the marble.**

ABOVE: **The French sculptor J.P. Filippi coaxes subtle shapes out of a snow-white piece of Carrara marble.**

RIGHT: **The Apuan Alps are most famous for the Carrara marble quarries, but their ancient silent forests and secret vales have a power all their own. Beneath the woodland slopes lie untapped miles of marble.**

OPPOSITE: **The atmospheric *crete senesi* of central Tuscany, near Siena, are sobering landscapes after the lush, tended fields and bustling cities. The virtually impermeable clay soil is vulnerable to dramatic erosion, which leaves stark white patches on the soft hillsides. The tenacious scrub, however, is perfect for grazing sheep.**

ABOVE: **A rosebush leavens the green of grapevines and the brown of soil and stubble in Montalcino. This horse demonstrates good taste: the vineyards of Montalcino are world-famous.**

LEFT: **A scraggly coastal pine and the dark green brush of the macchia set off the blue expanse of the Tyrrhenian Sea, near the lively port city of Leghorn. This stretch of the Mediterranean was named for the Tyrrenoi, the Etruscans, who as legend relates, emigrated from Asia Minor when years of famine had left their country famished. The Etruscans were an adventurous seafaring people, but were nonetheless cautious enough to live well inland. This coast, once prey to pirates, is today more peaceably invaded by vacationers.**

ABOVE AND OPPOSITE: **An aristocratic resort in Roman days and again today, Monte Argentario witnessed—and suffered through—dramatic events in Italy's history. In 1241, the Holy Roman emperor Frederick II destroyed the Genovese Guelph fleet bearing prelates to the ecumenical council convoked by Pope Gregory IX against the emperor. Some two hundred years later, the area was occupied by Alfonso V of Aragon; this *casale spagnolo*, or "Spanish homestead" (above), at Tómbolo della Giannella, dates from that era.**

OPPOSITE: **A spontaneous study in color: Portoferraio's sixteenth-century lighthouse peeps over the Tuscan roofs of this classic courtyard.**

BELOW: **Named for the iron that was the source of Elba's wealth in antiquity, Portoferraio was more recently home to Napoleon during his brief exile on the island.**

ABOVE: **Like the Camargue of southern France, the Maremma has a cowboy culture all its own. This *buttero* readies his tack for riding.**

LEFT: **This narrow promontory on Elba points into the Mediterranean like a ship heading out to sea. On islands or inland, tillable soil never goes to waste; resembling gardens more than fields, these few yards will furnish the local community with the savory ingredients of Tuscan seaside cuisine.**

ABOVE: **Brightly painted to be easy to spot from shore, these dinghies will ply the waters of the Tyrrhenian, as vessels have been doing since the late Stone Age.**

ABOVE: **Life provides endless opportunities for observation and commentary. The leisure to muse with old comrades is a pleasure that gives each day its flavor.**

RIGHT: **On a collective fishing boat at Elba, practiced hands join in an ancient choreography of gestures.**

ABOVE: **Fishing nets dream over the Arno River at Pisa, recalling the city's golden age as one of the great ports of the Mediterranean.**

ABOVE: Known for millennia as a source of mineral wealth, Elba has been home to successive waves of invaders—including Romans, Pisans, Genoese, Spanish, Turkish, and French—eager to secure those precious resources. Today, the island enjoys a reputation as an ideal location for a summer's idyl. At one point little more than a fishing village, the Marciana Marina (seen here at sunset) is now a stunning resort town that dreams among magnolias, palms, and oleanders as it gazes north out onto the Tyrrhenian Sea.

PAGE 96: **Cortona, in eastern Tuscany, perches on a series of small peaks offering some of the best views of the region. Here, the Chinese red of poppies and the shimmering silver of olive trees flutter in summer breezes as they have for thousands of years.**

PHOTO CREDITS